COPING



# HOMELESSNESS

ALEX NOVAK

ROSEN PUBLISHING

Published in 2023 by The Rosen Publishing Group, Inc.
2544 Clinton Street, Buffalo, NY 14224



Designer: Rachel Rising
Editor: Corona Brezina

Portions of this work were originally authored by Marcia Amidon Lusted and published as *Coping with Homelessness*. All new material in this edition was authored by Alex Novak.



**Library of Congress Cataloging-in-Publication Data**

Names: Novak, Alex, 1976- author.
Title: Homelessness / Alex Novak.
Description: Buffalo, NY : Rosen Publishing, [2023] | Series: Coping | Includes index.
Identifiers: LCCN 2022028487 (print) | LCCN 2022028488 (ebook) | ISBN 9781499473728 (library binding) | ISBN 9781499473711 (paperback) | ISBN 9781499473735 (ebook)
Subjects: LCSH: Homelessness--United States. | Homeless youth--United States--Social conditions.
Classification: LCC HV4505 .N69 2023 (print) | LCC HV4505 (ebook) | DDC 362.5/920973--dc23/eng/20220616
LC record available at https://lccn.loc.gov/2022028487
LC ebook record available at https://lccn.loc.gov/2022028488

Some of the images in this book illustrate individuals who are models. The depictions do not imply actual situations or events.

*Manufactured in the United States of America*

CPSIA Compliance Information: Batch #CSRYA23. For further information contact Rosen Publishing at 1-800-237-9932.

# CONTENTS

# CHAPTER 1

# HOMELESS IN AMERICA

Homelessness is a highly visible social issue. Homeless people are a common sight in public places in cities. They can be seen huddled in doorways or mingling among groups living in tent cities. But these unsheltered people are among the minority of the homeless population in the United States. Most homeless people are sheltered, meaning that they spend their nights in an emergency shelter or transitional housing.

Homelessness is a complex problem with no single root cause and no easy solution. The issue is frequently referred to as the "homelessness crisis." Each homeless person has their own story about how they became homeless. Likewise, no single approach can be guaranteed to help people escape homelessness. Observers sometimes tend to blame homeless people for making bad decisions that led to homelessness, but more often, their situation is the result of factors such as financial pressures or medical crises. The trauma experienced as they become homeless and endure homelessness makes it even more difficult for them to recover.

## WHO IS HOMELESS?

According to the United States Department of Housing and Urban Development (HUD), on a single night in 2020, about 580,000 people were homeless. Of this group, 61 percent were staying in emergency shelters or other forms of transitional housing, while 39 percent were unsheltered. Of these, 34,000 were youth under the age of 25 surviving on their own, 90 percent of them between the ages of 18 and 24.

A shortage of affordable housing is a leading cause of homelessness. Families may be at risk of becoming homeless when they can't manage to make rent or mortgage payments.

Homelessness includes people of every age, from children to the elderly, and both employed and unemployed people. About one-third suffers from mental illness, including schizophrenia, bipolar disorder, and depression. Twenty-one percent are considered chronically homeless, and 8 percent are veterans. About 53 percent are homeless in cities, 22 percent homeless in the suburbs, and 20 percent homeless in rural areas

Homeless teens can sometimes be seen panhandling for money on the streets. Some court rulings have found that panhandling qualifies as free speech, meaning that it can't be banned by law.

Beyond these groups, the people most at risk for becoming homeless are those living below the poverty level, the working poor (people who can't earn enough to survive), single-parent families, people recently released from prison, and teens who have gotten too old for the foster care system. The elderly are also a growing homeless population as they lose jobs or benefits or become ill and unable to work. Women and children are the fastest-growing population of homeless people, often because of abusive or economic situations.

## TALLYING THE HOMELESS

Counting the homeless is a difficult prospect. Every year, organizations working with the homeless conduct a Point-in-Time (PIT) count of the homeless, usually during the last 10 days of January. Volunteers collect some basic demographic information from people staying in shelters and living unsheltered. The data is used to help measure progress in ending homelessness and allocate resources in the future. The PIT count has been criticized, however, because it only provides a one-day snapshot of the homeless population. Cold and severe weather can also complicate the survey and skew the results in some regions.

Volunteers survey sheltered and unsheltered homeless people during the Point-in-Time (PIT) count. The data collected each year helps communities connect the homeless with housing and services.

In 2020, the count found that homelessness increased overall, continuing a four-year trend.

According to HUD, homeless people can also be categorized by how long they have been homeless. For example, disabled people who have been continually homeless for a year, or homeless for at least four episodes in three years, are called chronically homeless. There are also chronically homeless families. The chronically homeless are not the largest percentage of the homeless population, but they use more of the available services than people in other homeless categories.

Anyone younger than the age of 18 who is homeless and without adult supervision is classified as an unaccompanied youth. Those who are younger than the age of 20 and are parents or legal guardians of young children are referred to as parenting youth, and together they make up a parenting youth household. Young women who become pregnant and give birth while homeless are some of the most vulnerable people in the homeless population.

## WHERE ARE THEY?

HUD divides homelessness into four categories, which are used in determining eligibility for aid. The first category includes those who are living in a place that is not meant for humans to inhabit, such as bus stations, abandoned buildings, or alleys. It also includes homeless people who are living in emergency shelters or in transitional housing (housing meant to transition them from one situation to another), or people who are leaving prisons, mental health facilities, or other institutions.

The second category of homelessness includes those people who are losing their primary home where they spend days and nights. This might mean that the residence was a hotel or motel or a situation where the person was "doubled up," or living with someone by sleeping on their floor or couch.

The third category is people who live in unstable situations, especially families with children or unaccompanied youth. These situations might include people living in a rental property that is condemned for its uninhabitable conditions or with a family member who might kick them out at any time.

Homeless people may try to find shelter in places that are unsafe for human habitation, such as in derelict buildings or close to busy traffic near the street.

Finally, the fourth category is people who are running from domestic violence situations. They may have escaped violence permanently, or they are constantly running away from abusive partners who are still trying to find them.

## WHY ARE THEY HOMELESS?

Poverty is the biggest root cause of homelessness. There are a limited number of affordable housing units and housing assistance programs. The demand for these programs is much greater than the available supply. People who live in poverty are forced to make hard choices about where to spend their money. Even if they have jobs, those jobs may not pay enough to cover housing, food, child care, health care, and education. Since housing is often the biggest portion of a family's budget, it is often the first thing that must be given up when there isn't enough money.

There are other factors that contribute to homelessness. If individuals or families can't afford good health care, all it takes is one serious illness, accident, or disability to make it impossible to work. They deplete their savings to pay their medical bills, and eventually they can no longer pay rent or a mortgage and are evicted. Mental illness is also a strong contributor to homelessness, as people who suffer from it often cannot work and don't receive the medical care they need to stabilize their conditions. They may even have a damaged ability to accept help when it is offered. Addiction to drugs or alcohol can also contribute to homelessness because an addiction can consume a great deal of money and cause chronic health problems. Addicted people may be in and out of jail, and addiction also makes it difficult to keep a job.

Domestic violence is also a factor in homelessness. Women may have to make a choice between being in an abusive relationship and becoming homeless—sometimes they don't have any other housing options. The decision can be particularly difficult when children are involved. Landlords are more likely to evict victims of domestic violence due to a zero-tolerance policy for crime, regardless of whether the individual is the victim or perpetrator. They may also be unwilling to rent to victims of domestic violence, and women who have suffered domestic violence may have poor credit or employment history due to their situation. Women who live in poverty are more likely to suffer domestic violence as well as be more vulnerable to experiencing homelessness.

Unstable family situations can also be a factor in homelessness of children and young adults. Family conflict can lead to young people running away or being thrown out of the home. Some teenagers are at risk of homelessness when they turn 18 and "age out" of the foster care system. They no longer receive services from the state and often do not have the resources or skills to support themselves. Teens aging out of foster care are less likely to finish high school or attend college, and children of any age experiencing homelessness are at higher risk of mental health issues and academic difficulties.

Even when a woman is ready to leave an abusive relationship, she may have difficulty finding emergency shelter or transitional housing for herself and her family.

## MYTHS & FACTS

**MYTH:** Many homeless people are criminals with a potential for violence.

**FACT:** Homeless people are more likely to have a history with the criminal justice system, but the reason is often the criminalization of some aspects of homelessness. Examples include being ticketed for low-level offenses such as loitering, camping illegally, panhandling, or public urination. Despite high-profile stories about violent crimes by the homeless, homeless people are not more likely to commit violent crimes. Homeless people are actually more likely than the general public to be the victims of crime.

**MYTH:** All homeless people are addicted to drugs and alcohol.

**FACT:** According to the Substance Abuse and Mental Health Services Administration, about 38 percent of homeless people were dependent on alcohol and 26 percent abused other drugs. Substance abuse is usually not the cause of homelessness. In fact, substance abuse can be a consequence of homelessness rather than a cause. Homeless people may turn to drugs or alcohol to cope with their situation, and it's easy to obtain illegal drugs on the street.

**MYTH:** Homeless people could improve their situation if they just got a job.

**FACT:** Over half of the adults living in shelters reported earnings during the year that they were homeless, as did about 40 percent of those living unsheltered. Having a job does not guarantee enough income to cover the high cost of housing. Many homeless people also receive some form of government assistance, but it is still not adequate to pay for permanent housing. Being without a permanent home address and without clean clothes, a computer, a cell phone, and reliable transportation can make it very hard to get a job, and the homeless have higher rates of disability.

CHAPTER 2

# A LONG HISTORY OF HOMELESSNESS

Homelessness isn't a new problem in the United States. Before European settlers arrived, property and resources in North America were commonly owned. As far back as the colonial days in the 1640s, however, there have been people who could not afford housing. Sometimes, they were helped by their communities. Other times, they were considered vagrants and cast out from society. Poverty was considered a sign of a moral flaw, demonstrated by God punishing the poor for having a poor character. This pattern of blaming the homeless for their own situation continues into the modern day, although the rationalizations have changed with the times.

Back then, people believed that giving aid to the poor discouraged them from working. Although there were some exceptions, such as veterans, the poor had to work for any assistance. Children as young as age three had to perform some work.

## AUCTIONING OFF THE POOR

In colonial America, the support of poor people was the responsibility of the town that they lived in, rather than the state or federal government. The law said that no individual or family could be left to starve. A town might provide funds for poor families to keep living in their own homes or in rented rooms or houses. But if that family came to the point where they could no longer maintain their own home, even with the town's help, then the next step was to find them a place to live by auctioning them off.

During the town's annual town meeting, which was a form of democratic government in the towns of New England, the name of the head of the impoverished family was brought up in front of the town. It was noted how many people were in the family and what their ages were. Once they had this information, the male voting residents of the town would bid on the family's care. This meant that they would present an amount of money that they would be paid by the town in exchange for bringing the poor family into their own home and taking care of them. The lowest bidder would take on the care of that family for the next year.

Unfortunately, this system meant that poor families often lived in terrible conditions and did not have enough to eat. Eventually, towns replaced the auctioning off of the poor with the creation of "poor farms," farms that the town maintained where the poor would live and work.

## INDUSTRIALIZATION AND WAR

A new kind of homelessness came from the Industrial Revolution. As people began leaving farms and rural areas to find jobs in the cities and their factories, they often had no place to live. Often, going to jail was the only way to find shelter and food. Factory work also brought with it greater possibilities for injury and death because there were few safety regulations or precautions. Workers who were badly hurt or disabled had no safety net to rely on, and if they died, their widows and children would be left without any means of support. They might be evicted from their homes, and it was also a time when parents or other providers began to kick teens and young adults out of their homes because they could not afford to care for them.

The Civil War brought more homelessness with it. Many homes were destroyed in the South during the war. Medical science had also progressed to the point where badly injured men could survive but be too maimed or disabled to work. They often suffered from what is now called post-traumatic stress disorder (PTSD). The painkiller morphine had also been discovered and was easily available, bringing with it one of the first types of addiction. This epidemic of drug abuse led to the first criminalization of drug addiction, as well as creating a group of people whose addictions prevented them from living normal lives and supporting themselves.

One of the causes (and sometimes consequences) of homelessness is drug abuse. Some Civil War veterans became addicted to morphine, which is derived from the opium poppy plant.

Finally, a series of natural disasters took place between the end of the Civil War and the Great Depression, including the Great Chicago Fire, the 1906 San Francisco earthquake, the flooding of the Mississippi River, and droughts. All of these disasters increased homelessness either by totally destroying homes or livelihoods or by leaving victims disabled and with no resources for survival.

On April 18, 1906, a massive earthquake left San Francisco, California, devastated. Three thousand people were killed and half of the city's 400,000 residents were made homeless.

## ECONOMIC PRESSURES

In 1929, the United States entered a period known as the Great Depression, an economic crisis that lasted until World War II. During that time, unemployment was as high as 25 percent, meaning that one in four people did not have a job. As a result, many people could not pay their bills, including rent, mortgages, and taxes, and found themselves homeless. Some moved in with relatives, while others "squatted" in abandoned buildings, meaning that they lived in places without permission. Some homeless individuals and families built shanties out of whatever materials they could scavenge, such as scraps of wood and metal. Whole communities of these shanties were built. These areas became known as Hoovervilles because many people felt that President Hoover was responsible for the economic crisis that had occurred.

In the 1960s and 1970s, a contributor to homelessness was a trend toward deinstitutionalizing mentally ill people. Many were discharged from mental health institutions and treatment centers. These patients often did not receive enough follow-up community-based care after their release, and they became homeless because of their illnesses and their inability to cope.

The Hooverville in Seattle, Washington, housed 1,200 people and covered 9 acres (3.6 hectares) of land. It existed from 1931 to 1941.

Finally, those who grew up in poverty are said to be living in generational poverty. They have never known any other life, and since their families have been poor for many generations, there are no resources or support to receive further education and move out of poverty. These families get stuck in a cycle of poverty that often leads to homelessness.

## FIGHTING HOMELESSNESS

While homelessness has been present throughout American history, there have also been many attempts to help the homeless. In 1948, the United Nations adopted the Universal Declaration of Human Rights. Article 25 of the declaration stated that housing qualified as a basic human right. In 1968, the U.S. Congress passed a bill for an addition to the Civil Rights Act of 1964. The addition was known as the Fair Housing Act, and it prohibited discrimination in renting or selling housing based on race, gender, color, religion, or national origin. The act was intended to help people secure housing when they may previously have been rejected from renting or owning their own home.

One of the most important steps toward helping the homeless was the McKinney-Vento Act of 1987. This was the first piece of legislation specifically created to address the problem of homelessness. Before it, most of the response to homelessness was created on a local level, but people around the country began advocating for national attention to the problem. In 1986, the Homeless Persons' Survival Act was introduced in Congress. It included preventative actions, emergency measures, and long-term solutions to the problem of homelessness. However, only parts of the act ever became law: an act that no longer required someone to have a home address to receive benefits, and an act that created the Emergency Shelter Grants program and a transitional housing program, both of which were run by the U.S. Department of Housing and Urban Development (HUD). Finally, in 1986, the first part of the Homeless Persons' Survival Act passed, renamed the McKinney-Vento Act after the two congressmen who had led the fight for the act. It contains nine sections, called titles, which cover issues such as emergency shelters, transitional housing, health care, education, job training, and some permanent housing. It has been amended four times to add to or modify the original titles.

## HOMELESSNESS IN THE 21ST CENTURY

Many people who are homeless today owe their circumstances to the mortgage crisis that began in 2007. The crisis happened because too many people, including those who really couldn't afford a mortgage, were borrowing money to buy homes. Everyone assumed that housing prices would only go up, so buying a house would mean making a profit if it was sold a few years later. People who already had mortgages were taking out second mortgages, yet the wages for most jobs were not going up.

When housing prices stopped rising and interest rates on certain kinds of mortgages rose, many people could no longer afford their payments. Banks foreclosed on their homes, and soon there were too many empty bank-owned houses. Banks and investors began to fail because they had lent too

Between 2007 and 2010, about 3.8 million owners lost their homes to foreclosure—the process in which a borrower loses a home to the bank due to failure to repay a mortgage.

## HOMELESS IN THE PANDEMIC

When the COVID-19 pandemic struck in the spring of 2020, some advocates feared that the pandemic could be devastating for the homeless. Many homeless people have underlying health conditions that could leave them more vulnerable to the virus. Conditions at shelters make social distancing difficult, and some public places became inaccessible during lockdowns. In addition, the homeless often lack reliable access to medical care. As the pandemic affected the economy, some areas saw an increase in demand for services for the homeless.

As it turned out, the pandemic did not cause a COVID crisis leading to high case numbers and deaths among the homeless. Death rates did rise among the homeless in the two years following the beginning of the pandemic, although COVID was not found to be the direct cause. Most of the increase in deaths was attributed to drug overdoses. However, the pandemic likely was a contributing factor. The health care system was strained during the pandemic, and some services such as substance abuse treatment were disrupted. People, including the homeless, felt stressed, anxious, and helpless during the pandemic, and overall rates of drug use and abuse increased. The result has been record high levels of overdose deaths, with high rates among the homeless exacerbating the overall homelessness crisis in the United States.

much money. At the same time, the U.S. economy was no longer growing and prices were rising. Many people lost their homes to foreclosure and became homeless. Though some may still have had jobs, they were now unable to afford their homes.

Crisis struck in 2020 with the onset of the COVID-19 pandemic. The next years were marked by economic turmoil and social unrest along with a disruption of everyday life. Millions of people lost their jobs in the months immediately after the start of the pandemic, but an unprecedented economic stimulus prevented many workers from sliding into poverty. A strong labor market has provided opportunities for many people who may have otherwise struggled to find employment, but soaring home prices have increased the cost of housing. Disruptions to social services for the homeless and the annual PIT count of the homeless have left an unclear picture of the overall impact of the ongoing pandemic on the homeless.

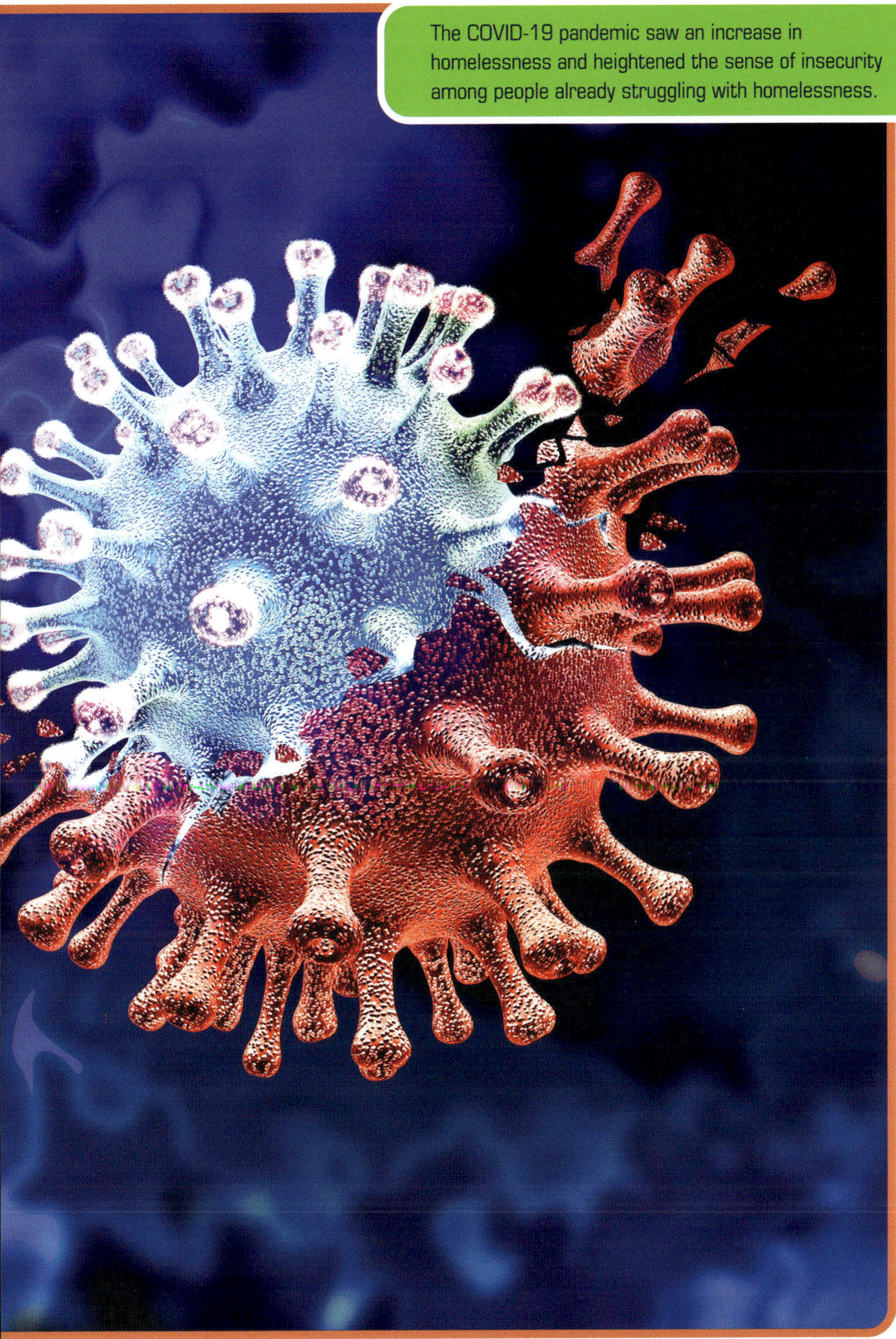

The COVID-19 pandemic saw an increase in homelessness and heightened the sense of insecurity among people already struggling with homelessness.

CHAPTER 3

# YOUTH HOMELESSNESS

There's no age limit for homelessness. Every year, 4.2 million children and young adults experience homelessness. About 700,000 of these are unaccompanied minors—young people under the age of 24 who are not accompanied by a parent or guardian, and are not part of a family. (Different organizations use different age ranges and criteria to define "homeless youth.") About 30 percent of the homeless in the United States are under the age of 24.

Moreover, many homeless advocates report that the numbers of homeless youth are undercounted. Homeless youth often qualify as the "hidden homeless" who lack a permanent home but don't live unsheltered or in shelters. Instead, they temporarily stay in other people's homes or even in motels. Often, they hide their homeless status from teachers and other authorities due to the stigma attached to homelessness.

## ROOT CAUSES

The reasons why teens find themselves homeless fall into three categories, which are all connected. Teen homelessness can be caused by family problems, economic problems, and unstable housing situations.

Family problems can cover a wide range of situations. Teens may experience physical or emotional abuse from a parent or a parent's partner until they reach the point where they run away either for self-preservation or because they can no longer tolerate the abuse. A study by the U.S. Department of Health and Human Services found that 46 percent of runaway and homeless youth had been physically abused and 17 percent had experienced unwanted sexual activity by a family or household member. Drug and alcohol addiction also play a major role in driving teens from their homes or as a reason why parents become abusive. Often, an addicted parent will be arrested and incarcerated, leaving teens with no means of support. Addicted parents or caregivers may also neglect children and teens in their care, failing to provide enough food or clothing or a safe placc to livc.

Being a teenager or young adult means seeking independence and questioning authority, and in most families, this is a natural process that parents and teens work through together. But teens who rebel against their parents' authority might also find that they are no longer welcome in their own home. These strained family relationships may lead to a teen being kicked out by parents, running away from rebellion, or a desire for independence and freedom of choice.

Another issue that drives teens and young adults from their homes is sexual orientation or gender identity. LGBTQ+ (lesbian, gay, bisexual, transgender, or questioning) youth are twice as likely as their non-LGBTQ+ peers

LGBTQ+ youth are more likely to become homeless than their non-LGBTQ+ peers. Living unsheltered, they're also at a high risk of physical and sexual exploitation.

to experience homelessness. It is estimated that LGBTQ+ teens make up as much as 40 percent of all homeless youth, even though they only represent 7 percent of the general population. In particular, Black LGBTQ+ teens are twice as likely as white LGBTQ+ young adults to be homeless.

The leading reason for homeless LGBTQ+ youth is family rejection resulting from their sexual or gender identity. Some also report being subjected to physical, emotional, or sexual abuse. When seeking

## DEFINING HOMELESS YOUTH

The McKinney-Vento Act of 1987 provides the official definition of the term "homeless children and youth" under federal law:

Individuals who lack a fixed, regular, and adequate nighttime residence . . .; and includes—

- Children and youths who are sharing the housing of other persons due to loss of housing, economic hardship, or a similar reason; are living in motels, hotels, trailer parks, or camping grounds due to the lack of alternative adequate accommodations; are living in emergency or transitional shelters; are abandoned in hospitals; or are awaiting foster care placement;
- Children and youths who have a primary nighttime residence that is a public or private place not designed for or ordinarily used as a regular sleeping accommodation for human beings...
- Children and youths who are living in cars, parks, public spaces, abandoned buildings, substandard housing, bus or train stations, or similar settings; and
- Migratory children who qualify as homeless.

housing, LGBTQ+ youth are sometimes asked to leave shelters because of their sexual orientation or gender identity. As a result, they are more likely than non-LGBTQ+ young adults to end up living unsheltered.

Eviction leading to homelessness can be traumatic for every member of a family, leading to physical and mental health consequences along with financial uncertainty.

## FINANCIAL TROUBLES

Another factor that families may struggle with, and one that often leads to teen homelessness, is money. Many families are facing home foreclosure, bankruptcy, huge amounts of debt, and unemployment. A family's economic circumstances can lead to situations where teens become a burden. The wages of the working adults may be too low to live on, or if the family receives benefits like welfare, they might be insufficient.

Death or job loss can also devastate a family's finances. If a family lives in poverty, they may tell their teens to move out when they reach the age of 18, simply because they cannot afford another person to feed, shelter, and clothe. Eighteen-year-olds may be considered old enough to fend for themselves, but this often disrupts their chances of a good education. Some teens are kicked out by their parents because they have mental health issues that the family cannot afford to treat. Teens with solid family relationships may become homeless along with their parents, but then leave to go off on their own.

When families struggle to pay for basic necessities such as rent, utilities, food, healthcare, and transportation, a single financial emergency can tip them toward homelessness.

Teens who have been incarcerated in a juvenile detention facility for committing crimes, in mental health institutions, or in the foster care system may become homeless when they are released from these kinds of institutions at the age of 18. This is referred to as "aging out" because once they reach this age, they are no longer considered to be minors and are no longer eligible for programs that help children. Foster children, in particular, may be brutally ripped from lives where they have been going to school and doing well. Foster kids who age out of the system also lose their support system of adults and family at a critical time in their lives, which can have drastic consequences. As stated by the organization Child Trends, the statistics for teens aging out of foster care are grim:

- One in four will be involved in the criminal justice system within the first two years after they leave the system.
- More than one-fifth will become homeless at some time after age 18.
- Approximately 58 percent had a high school degree at age 19, compared to 87 percent of a national comparison group of non-foster youth.
- Of youth who aged out of foster care and are older than the age of 25, fewer than 3 percent earned their college degrees, compared with 28 percent of the general population.

Foster children who "age out" of the system are at a higher risk of homelessness because they lack support from either their families or government programs.

Transitions are even more difficult for teens released from juvenile detention or a mental health facility because they are often not prepared to survive on their own after years of being sheltered and fed.

## SERIOUS CONSEQUENCES

Teens face many problems when they become homeless, whether they are living in a shelter or on the street. Mental health issues are common, such as anxiety and depression, as well as low self-esteem. Teens may act out with abusive behaviors, like self-harming, or even attempt suicide. These issues, as well as stress and desperation, can lead to substance abuse with alcohol or drugs.

Homeless teens may also commit crimes to survive or become victims of crimes themselves because they are vulnerable. Others resort to prostitution and unsafe sexual practices. This kind of "survival sex" means they are trading sex for money, shelter, or drugs. It can lead to diseases and pregnancy, especially with a lack of access to birth control or health care, and homeless teens have a higher rate of pregnancy than the general population. Other health problems related to homelessness include poor nutrition and untreated illnesses, as well as HIV and AIDS. And death is always a possibility from any of these factors.

Finally, homeless teens are often unable to complete high school and are unlikely to go on to attend college. Even if a youth manages to attend school regularly, they may lack complete school records necessary for enrolling in higher education. The McKinney-Vento Act includes a section on education for homeless youth that aims to reduce barriers to enrollment and provide services such as referrals for health or housing resources. Nonetheless, homelessness often leads to young people lacking the education and skills to find solid jobs that will enable them to overcome their circumstances.

As many as 20 percent of homeless young women become pregnant, but few organizations provide services for pregnant and parenting teens.

# CHAPTER 4

# SURVIVING HOMELESSNESS

For teens, homelessness is marked by instability and risk. Homelessness is an awful condition for any human being, but children and young adults lack adult judgment and decision-making skills. The adolescent brain isn't fully mature until about the age of 25. As a result, teens are less prepared to cope with homelessness and more likely to be damaged by trauma and stress experienced while homeless. Homelessness interrupts regular routines of school, social activities, and family life. Homeless youth surviving on their own are vulnerable to a range of threats. They may face inadequate food and housing. They may suffer from untreated mental or physical health issues or substance abuse. Homeless youth can be subject to assault and victimization, and they are at a higher risk of suicide than their peers.

## SEEKING SHELTER

Shelter is the most important thing for a homeless teen to find. The best place to start is close to home: they should try to find a relative or a friend who will provide a place to stay, even if just temporarily. Even a college-aged friend who will share a dorm room or a couch in an apartment is a better option than being on the streets. It is important, in the case of staying with a teenaged friend, that their parents are aware of the homeless teen's presence and agree to it. Teens who belong to a church may also find that it provides resources for people who need to find shelter.

If staying with relatives or friends is not an option, teens can look for open beds at a shelter or pay a minimal amount to stay in a youth hostel or a YMCA. Teens with cars may have to live in them temporarily, but if they are forced to live on the streets, public

In warm-weather California, 70 percent of the homeless population lives unsheltered. Over 50 percent of all unsheltered homeless Americans live in California.

places like libraries, bus stations, and transportation centers are warmer and safer than the street. Riding a subway or bus is also a way to stay warm for a while. Warehouses and abandoned buildings should be considered a last resort as a place to take shelter. Camping in a tent in a park or other public outside area is an option during warmer weather. Teens should avoid any arrangement in which staying with someone is in exchange for sex or other favors.

## UNCERTAIN SHELTER

In 2020, the number of people living unsheltered rose 7 percent. Helping get people off of the streets is a priority for many organizations, but there is a shortage of beds in shelters in many states. Another factor is that some homeless people prefer to stay out of shelters. There are various reasons for this preference. The homeless may have valid concerns about safety and health. People have reported being assaulted or abused in shelters, especially women, and there have been cases of pest infestations and disease transmission in homeless shelters. People in shelters are often separated by sex, which might not be acceptable for couples, families, or transgender people. Families may be broken up. Pets are usually not allowed. Homeless people may have jobs with hours that conflict with a shelter's opening and closing times. Also, shelters are temporary living situations that don't provide people with a place to keep personal possessions or offer a sense of security that they'll be welcome the next day.

## BASIC NEEDS

For homeless teens who are still enrolled in school, it is likely that they can be enrolled in free breakfast and lunch programs, giving them at least two solid meals a day. Other options include going to soup kitchens and free meal programs sponsored by homeless shelters or food pantries. Some teens will panhandle, meaning that they ask for donations from people on the street and use that money to purchase food. "Dumpster diving" for discarded food behind restaurants is not safe because spoiled food can cause illness, and most homeless teens cannot easily get medical care.

Free school lunches provide millions of needy children and teens with nutritious food. Homeless youth can also get meals from food pantries and soup kitchens.

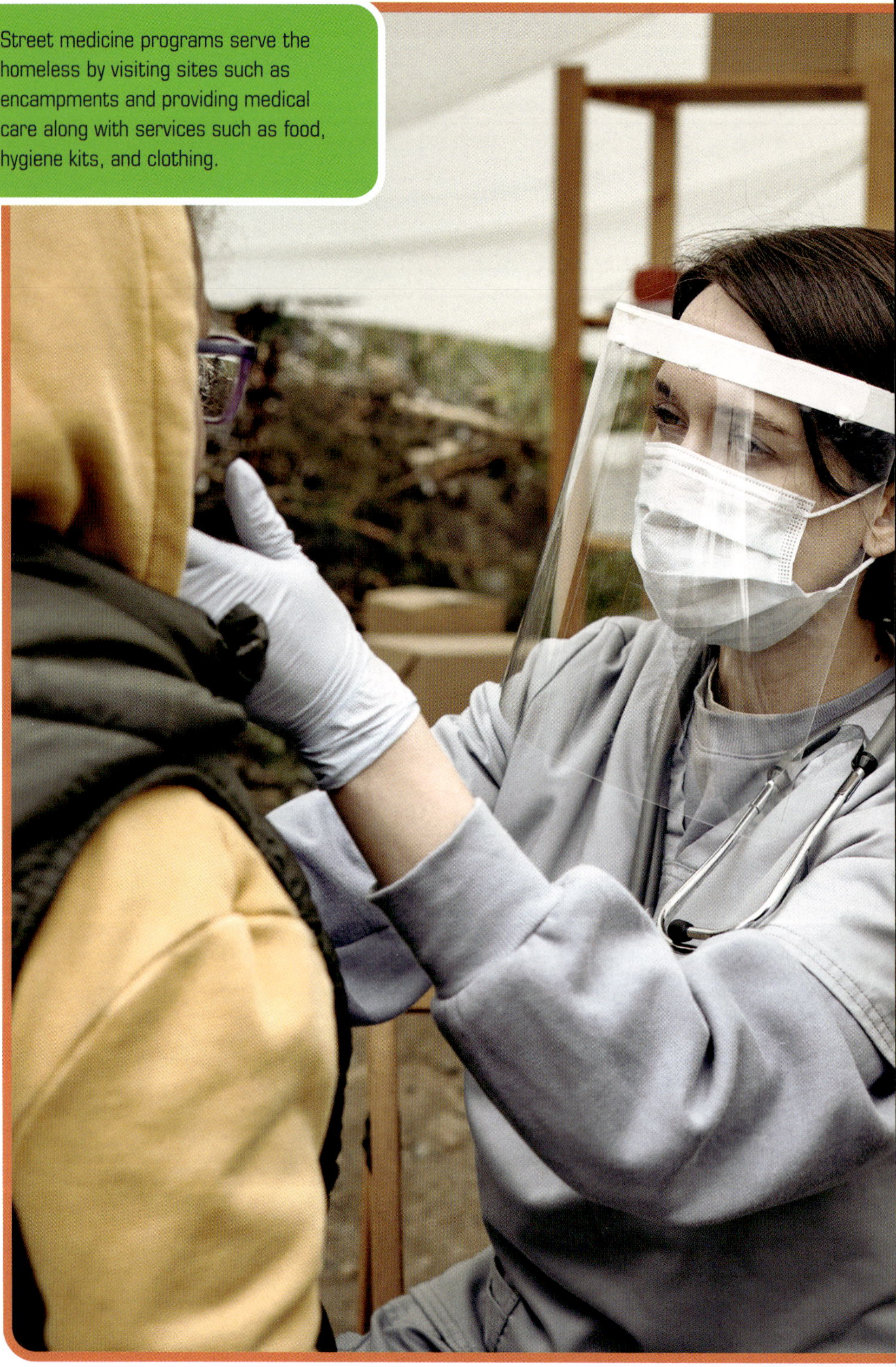

Street medicine programs serve the homeless by visiting sites such as encampments and providing medical care along with services such as food, hygiene kits, and clothing.

Schools are also useful for personal hygiene because locker rooms usually have shower facilities. Many shelters and assistance organizations provide free toiletries to the homeless, and some shelters may allow them to use shower facilities even if they do not stay there. Clothing, which is vital for staying warm in colder climates, is often also available from shelters and clothing donation organizations. Churches may also provide used clothing and warm coats.

Medical care can be more difficult to find. Many towns and cities maintain free clinics where homeless people can walk in and receive care. Some cities are starting to have mobile vans that provide free medical care at various places each day, on a schedule that allows for follow-up care from one week to the next. Finally, it is important to maintain contact. Social media is a good tool for staying in touch with friends and family and can be accessed from free library computers. A cell phone is very valuable because it also provides a stable phone number to use when looking for a job, as well as access to teen homelessness hotlines.

It's possible for a teen to survive on the street, but not to thrive. A homeless teen's best option is to seek safe and stable permanent housing. A teen may feel ashamed or wary of asking for help, whether from friends, family, or social service organizations. But there are resources available that will help young people get their lives together and reach their full potential, regardless of their circumstances.

Maintaining connections with friends and other social contacts can be critical to good mental health as well as a means of accessing resources to overcome homelessness.

# CHAPTER 5

# REACHING OUT

Many people describe their experience with homelessness as a downward spiral. Their problems begin with financial troubles. Sometimes, substance abuse, mental illness, or health issues are contributing factors. They may lose their job, fall behind on bills, lose their home, and arrange to stay with friends or family, but that's not a long-term solution. They may end up living in their car and then spending nights in homeless shelters. Some people reach the point where they live unsheltered on the streets for an occasional stretch, and then become chronically homeless.

Timothy Busby, a homeless writer who has experienced many of these stages of homelessness, urges his readers to adjust their perspective: "Treat those who are less fortunate than you are the same as you would like to be treated if you ever end up on the street."

## PRACTICAL HELP

What are the best ways to help the homeless people who are on the street every day? Surprisingly, one of the biggest things is to acknowledge the presence of homeless people and engage with them in a casual conversation. Homelessness can be corrosive to a person's self-worth, and it can be very lonely too. Often, a simple hello in passing can make a big difference in a person's day. For more tangible help, experts say that it's usually best to give gift cards for grocery stores or fast food restaurants, rather than cash. Small, nutritional food items like granola bars, as well as bottles of water, are also useful. Even buying a second cup of coffee in the morning and giving it to someone on the street is a gesture that is helpful.

In cold weather climates, it can also be helpful to give out warm clothing. It doesn't have to be new, but it could be serviceable clothing that is no longer useful or is the wrong size or color. Socks are always in high demand among the homeless. In warm weather climates, clean T-shirts and sun hats can make a big difference. Also, small-sized toiletries from hotels are also useful for peoplc living on the street.

One user on Reddit, a social media news website, asked for comments from formerly homeless people, asking how people could best help the homeless. One user responded: "When people ask homeless what do you need, they are thinking about objects, things like hats, socks and gloves or any other things useful in routine life. These objects make a small difference. But the most important things are not objects. Things that make the most impact and help someone are non-objects. Dignity. Kindness and understanding. Encouragement."

# TENT ENCAMPMENTS

It's a familiar sight in large cities: clusters of tents erected in parks or other open spaces, on roadsides, or beneath highway overpasses. Tent cities are found across the United States, and most tent encampments of homeless people do not have a legalized status. In some case, they are tolerated by authorities despite being unsanctioned. Often, they are considered a health and safety concern and are dismantled by the police.

Tent cities represent a vexing issue for policy makers. A root cause of the rise in encampments is a lack of affordable housing. Advocates for the homeless argue that although tent cities do not offer a long-term solution to homelessness, cities punish people for circumstances beyond their control when they sweep encampments. A common approach is "clearance and closure with support," as described in the 2020 report Exploring Homelessness Among People Living in Encampments and Associated Costs. Outreach workers work with residents to provide alternate means of housing before they leave the encampment. But in some cities and states with large homeless populations, such as Portland, Oregon, lawmakers have begun enacting stricter measures directed at the homeless as a result of business and community concerns.

Tent cities may appear to be an urban blight, but to many homeless, they represent a source of community otherwise lacking in their lives.

Efforts such as fundraisers and food drives can help the homeless and raise awareness among members of the community about their situation.

## VOLUNTEERING AND ADVOCACY

Another way to help the homeless is by volunteering for organizations that help them. Soup kitchens, shelters, food pantries, hotline programs, and church groups often need many extra hands, and donating time rather than material objects is a good way to help the homeless. These kinds of organizations are also a good place to donate money because it is more likely to be used to directly help the homeless. Some smaller towns and suburbs might also maintain special funds to quietly provide assistance to homeless citizens or people in danger of becoming homeless, and they also welcome donations.

If there aren't any organizations that help the homeless in a particular area, then it could be a good idea to start one. Teens can start projects in their schools or churches to collect used clothing or personal hygiene kits, or hold food drives for shelters and soup kitchens. They can also hold benefits to raise money for homeless organizations. You can also raise awareness of issues concerning the homeless by writing about homelessness in your community for your school newspaper. Learn about resources available to the homeless in your area, such as mental health services, housing assistance, low-cost health care, and shelters. Urge your local leaders and lawmakers to support these efforts.

## HAVE RESPECT

There are some things that people should not do when it comes to interacting with homeless people, especially on the street. They should not ignore them, even when they are asked for money. Homeless people may have already given up a great deal of pride to ask strangers for money, and by ignoring them, it perpetuates the feeling that homeless people are invisible to everyone else. It's better simply to say, "I'm sorry, I can't today." Never tell a homeless person to go get a job—many homeless people actually do have jobs, but their jobs don't pay enough for them to have housing. Never assume that someone sitting on the street asking for money is lying, even though some people think that homeless people

People tend to hold negative stereotypes about the homeless. Remind yourself to challenge your own preconceptions when you interact with homeless people.

get up at the end of the day and go home to comfortable houses. And never assume that homeless people are all criminals and drug users.

In the end, not all homeless people are the same or homeless for the same reasons. And while it is necessary to be careful when interacting with any stranger, it is also necessary to show basic human courtesy.

Homelessness is an ongoing crisis that persists due to a combination of economic and social factors. There's no guarantee that the situation will begin to improve in the short-term future. The actions of ordinary people can make a difference, however. It can be uncomfortable to see people experiencing homelessness, but you can take a few small but significant steps toward acknowledging their humanity and doing your best to help.

# CHAPTER 6

# ADDRESSING HOMELESSNESS

Most people who are homeless fell into their situation through circumstances beyond their control. The government and private organizations provide a safety net of resources such as rental assistance, shelter referrals, food aid, and low-cost health clinics. Most communities have a Continuum of Care (CoC) program that administers homeless services. One approach toward reducing homelessness is the "Housing First" model. The homeless are provided with housing with no preconditions such as employment or substance abuse treatment. The approach is based on the idea that people will be in a better position to improve their lives if they're already in a stable housing situation.

Homelessness may seem like the end of the line to someone who's desperate and in need. But it does not have to be. There are many people who move back out of homelessness and many organizations and resources to help them achieve that goal.

## FROM HOMELESS TO HARVARD

Dawn Loggins had just spent six weeks at a summer course for gifted students and was about to enter her senior year of high school when her parents abandoned her. Vivian Kuo described the story:

> [Dawn] kept calling her parents' phone, only to learn it had been disconnected. "When I returned, my grandmother had been dropped off at a local homeless shelter, my brother had just left, and my parents had just gone," she says. "I found out later they had moved to Tennessee." Her voice is steady, matter of fact. "I never expected my parents to just, like, leave."

Dawn slept on couches and floors at friends' houses. She didn't want to enter the social services system because she might be uprooted and forced to move around. Dawn was an excellent student and wanted to finish high school in her own school. The faculty at the school rallied around her and found her a place to live and a job as a custodian at the school. She could concentratc on school and her goal of going to college. She applied to five different schools, including Harvard, her dream school.

> Months passed. She was accepted to the four schools in North Carolina. Days went by. Nothing from Harvard.
>
> But on a sunny day earlier this year...there was a letter from Harvard, the type of letter every high school senior dreads from a university—a regular-sized envelope, the ominous sign of rejection. Cautiously, she opened it: "Dear Ms. Loggins, I'm delighted to report that the admissions committee has asked me to inform you that you

will be admitted to the Harvard College class of 2016...We send such an early positive indication only to outstanding applicants..."

She gasped when she read those words.

Dawn flourished at Harvard and graduated in May of 2016. In 2014, Business Insider named her one of its "19 Incredibly Impressive Students at Harvard." She also has a nonprofit organization to benefit other disadvantaged students and has raised more than $35,000.

Dawn's story is just one of hundreds showing how homeless teens and adults have found ways to move out of their circumstances and achieve their goals. Some are helped by friends and teachers, as Dawn was, but there are many other resources that can help homeless people move off the streets and back into productive, stable lives.

Dawn Loggins proved that homeless teens can move beyond their desperate situation and succeed. She excelled in school and was accepted at Harvard University.

## HUD ASSISTANCE

The United States government, through HUD, has many programs to help the homeless. The Continuum of Care (CoC) program promotes community involvement in helping homeless people and quickly rehousing them. It provides funding to nonprofits, as well as state and local governments, to accomplish this and to help homeless individuals and families become self-sufficient.

HUD also has an Emergency Shelter Grants program to provide funding for more emergency homeless shelters, as well as the Housing Opportunities for Persons with AIDS (HOPWA) program for people specifically suffering from HIV/AIDS. There is also the Title V program, which allows organizations such as homeless shelters to use surplus federal government property to assist homeless people. On January 13, 2017, HUD announced a new program, the Youth Homelessness Demonstration Program, which supplies funding to ten communities that are working to end youth homelessness. HUD also has programs to help people who have become homeless because

of the closing of military bases, in addition to a joint program with the U.S. Department of Veterans Affairs to provide housing vouchers and counseling specifically to military veterans, who make up a large portion of the homeless population. While all of HUD's programs are government-based, homeless people can visit its website to locate services available in their area and learn how to access them.

People at risk of homelessness can learn about programs funded by the U.S. Department of Housing and Urban Development (HUD) at www.hudexchange.info.

Covenant House provides homeless youth with housing and support such as health care and job training. The organization has locations across the country.

## COMMUNITY AID

For many homeless people, however, the most accessible kind of help comes from community organizations. These organizations come in two types: local branches of national (or even international) organizations and organizations that are entirely local and are created and run by local communities. National organizations include the National Coalition for the Homeless, which is "a national network of people who are currently experiencing or who have experienced homelessness, activists and advocates, community-based and faith-based service providers, and others committed to a single mission: to prevent and end homelessness while ensuring the immediate needs of those experiencing homelessness are met and their civil rights protected." The National Alliance to End Homelessness, Volunteers of America, Covenant House, and StandUp for Kids are other organizations with branches in many major American cities. There are also national service groups, such as the Lions Club, Kiwanis, or Rotary, that may have programs for helping the homeless.

Local community-based programs will vary from place to place. They may be more difficult to find, and it may require calling or visiting a social service agency or a city or town government office to find them. For homeless teens, visiting a school guidance office is another way to find resources and help. Many churches and synagogues also have outreach programs to help the homeless and the hungry. Again, it might be necessary to visit or call the specific church group and ask if they have assistance, but most clergy members are used to being asked for help and can at least guide homeless people in the right direction to get help.

The McKinney-Vento Act requires that every school district appoint a local homeless education liaison to ensure that the educational needs of homeless students are met.

## EMERGENCY SITUATIONS

For homeless people in dire situations who have an emergency medical condition or find themselves in a criminal or dangerous situation, the best thing to do is to call 911. Not only will emergency service personnel help with the immediate problem, but they will also know where to get additional assistance and what organizations and resources are available. Almost every national and many local organizations dedicated to helping the homeless also have hotlines that are answered 24 hours a day. These hotlines can provide immediate help, sometimes even sending out a van or an organization worker to get the homeless person and bring them to a shelter. In major metropolitan areas, these hotline numbers are often posted in places like bus stations and libraries, as well as in phone books (when they are still available). Anyone can find them on a computer in a public library or internet café or by using a cell phone.

In addition to general hotlines, there are resources for people experiencing specific situations such as domestic violence or homelessness as a veteran.

## OVERCOMING HOMELESSNESS

No matter what their circumstances, homeless individuals and families can always find some sort of help, and it often comes from unexpected sources: the kindness of strangers, not just the work of large organizations. When he was 19, Matthew Tejeda found himself checking into a homeless shelter in New York City. His story was told in a *Forbes* magazine article by Micah Solomon: "I carried a key in my pocket when I was homeless because I believed that one day I'd have my own place," he said. He was lucky to apply for a job at a coffee shop and find that the manager was willing to give him a chance, even when he explained that he was living in a shelter. Matthew got the job, but as it did not pay enough for him to afford the high city rents, he continued to live in the shelter for another year, which could be challenging: "One of the real challenges of this, while trying to hold down a job and better yourself, is that the shelter life—sleeping in a room with seven other guys and no enforced sleep schedule—means getting very little sleep. It's hard opening a [coffee]

store at 4:30 am off no sleep. Some nights that were really loud at the shelter, rather than lying sleepless in my bed, I'd lock myself in the bathroom for a couple of hours with my head against the wall to try and get a nap in before opening."

Homelessness is a complicated issue with no straightforward solution, but there are resources available for individuals through community and government programs.

In time, Matthew was promoted to assistant store manager and, for the first time, could afford his own apartment, with some help from an existing employee assistance fund through his store's parent company: "I got promoted and moved into my apartment in the same week. The first night in my apartment I cried my eyes out. For the first time in my entire life I knew exactly where I would sleep that night and the next night after that, and that sense of security did not depend on anything in the world except myself." He has since been made the manager at one of the chain's busiest locations, at New York's Penn Station. Matthew's story shows that someone who is homeless can successfully move out of unemployment and a shelter situation and into their own space and a successful life.

It's crucial that ordinary people take notice of the issue of homelessness and advocate for measures that have been proven to be effective.

# 10 GREAT QUESTIONS TO ASK A SOCIAL WORKER

1. Where can someone go for help if they're at risk of becoming homeless?

2. What resources and services are available to help the homeless?

3. Where can the homeless connect with job training and placement programs?

4. Where can homeless teens find shelters and organizations that can meet their needs?

5. What resources are available to help homeless teens succeed in school?

6. How does the legal system criminalize homelessness?

7. Do homeless people have the legal right to live on the streets and panhandle for money?

8. What should a homeless person do if he or she feels unsafe or threatened?

9. How can I help a friend or family member who's at risk of becoming homeless?

10. What can I do to help homeless people in my area?

No mattter how you take a stand against homelessness—whether helping out at a food drive or writing a letter to the editor—every effort makes a difference.

# GLOSSARY

**abusive** Involving violence or cruelty, either physically or verbally.

**addiction** The compulsive need for a substance like drugs or alcohol.

**bankruptcy** The state of being unable to repay debts.

**budget** An estimate of the income and expenses available for a certain period of time.

**chronic** Constantly reoccurring or lasting a long time.

**condemn** To judge a building as being unfit or even dangerous to live in or use.

**criminalization** Turning an activity into a criminal offense by making it illegal.

**democratic** Based on a form of government where people choose leaders by voting.

**deplete** To use up a supply of something, such as money.

**domestic** Having to do with a household or family relationships.

**economic** Relating to the earning, distribution, and use of money.

**eligible** Qualified to participate in or be chosen for something.

**evict** To remove someone from land or a building, often with the support of the law.

**guardian** Someone who is legally responsible for the care of another person.

**hygiene** A practice that has to do with staying clean and healthy.

**legislation** A law or set of laws made by a government.

**liaison** Someone who provides a connection between people or groups for the purpose of commnication and cooperation.

**mortgage** A long-term loan from a bank used to purchase a home.

**preconception** An idea or opinion that someone has before learning about something directly.

**transitional** In the process of changing from one situation or state to another.

**uninhabitable** Unsuitable to live in.

# FOR MORE INFORMATION

## CANADIAN OBSERVATORY ON HOMELESSNESS

Homeless Hub
York University
6th Floor, Kaneff Tower
4700 Keele St.
Toronto, ON M3J 1P3
(416) 736-2100 ext. 30208
Website: thehub@edu.yorku.ca
Facebook: @homelesshub
Twitter: @homelesshub
Instagram: @homelesshub

The Canadian Observatory on Homelessness is the largest national research institute devoted to homelessness in Canada. The COH is the curator of the Homeless Hub, which is a library of over 30,000 resources.

## COALITION FOR THE HOMELESS

129 Fulton Street
New York, NY 10038
(212) 776-2000
Website: www.coalitionforthehomeless.org
Facebook, Instagram: @nyhomeless
Twitter: @NYHomeless

The Coalition for the Homeless serves the homeless through programs providing food, housing assistance, job training, and crisis services. The organization also helps homeless youth and advocates for the rights of the homeless and for policies addressing the issue of homelessness.

## COVENANT HOUSE

Covenant House Headquarters
461 Eighth Avenue
New York, NY 10001
(800) 388-3888
Website: www.covenanthouse.org
Facebook: @CovenantHouse
Twitter: @CovenantHouse
Instagram: @Covenant_House
Covenant House provides programs and support designed to help young people experiencing homelessness through a network of more than 30 branch houses located in the United States, Canada, Mexico, and Latin America.

## FAMILY PROMISE

71 Summit Avenue
Summit, NJ 07901
(908) 273-1100
Website: familypromise.org
Facebook: @FamilyPromise
Twitter: @fpnational
Instagram: @family.promise
Family Promise focuses on finding innovative solutions to family homelessness through community-based programs that deliver shelter, prevention, and stabilization services.

## NATIONAL ALLIANCE TO END HOMELESSNESS

1518 K Street NW, 2nd Floor
Washington, D.C. 20005
(202) 638-1526
Website: endhomelessness.org
Facebook: @naehomelessness
Twitter: @naehomelessness
This alliance works to educate the public and lawmakers about homelessness, provides resources at the ground level to help the homeless, and offers guidance to improve public policies.

## RAISING THE ROOF

116 Industry Street, Suite 208
Toronto, ON M6M 4L8
Canada
(416) 481-1838
Website: www.raisingtheroof.org
Facebook: @RaisingtheRoof
Twitter: @RaisingTheRoof
Instagram: @raisingtheroofcanada
Raising the Roof partners with agencies throughout Canada to provide lasting solutions to homelessness through education and collaboration at the local level.

## TRUE COLORS UNITED

311 West Forty-Third Street, 12th Floor
New York, NY 10036
(212) 461-4401
Website: truecolorsunited.org
Facebook: @truecolorsunited
Twitter: @truecolorsunite
Instagram: @truecolorsunited
This organization offers safe and affirming services designed to help LGBTQ+ youth who are experiencing homelessness or at risk of becoming homeless.

# FOR FURTHER READING

Cartlidge, Cherese. *Homeless Youth*. San Diego, CA: ReferencePoint Press, 2017.

Erskine, H. Craig, III. *Teen Homelessness*. New York, NY: Greenhaven Publishing, 2018.

Graham, Alan. *Welcome Homeless: One Man's Journey of Discovering the Meaning of Home*. New York, NY: Thomas Nelson, 2017.

Kozol, Jonathan. *Rachel and Her Children: Homeless Families in America*. New York, NY: Broadway Books, 2006.

Lüsted, Marcia Amidon. *I Am Homeless. Now What?* New York, NY: Rosen Publishing, 2017.

New York Times Editorial Staff. *The Homeless: An Increasing Population*. New York, NY: New York Times Educational Publishing, 2020.

Sydner, Gail. *Homeless: Youth Living on the Streets*. San Diego, CA: ReferencePoint Press, 2021.

Toth, Henrietta. *Coping with Life in Homeless Shelters*. New York, NY: Rosen Publishing, 2019.

Uhl, Xina M. *Homelessness*. Rosen Verified: Current Issues. New York, NY: Rosen Publishing, 2021.

Wagner, David. *No Longer Homeless: How the Ex-homeless Get and Stay Off the Streets*. Lanham, MD: Rowman & Littlefield, 2020.

# INDEX

# ABOUT THE AUTHOR

**ALEX NOVAK** is a freelance writer who has written many nonfiction books for children and teens, many of them addressing issues teenagers face in their daily lives. She lives in New York.

# PHOTO CREDITS

Photo Credit: Cover,p. 5 Roman Bodnarchuk/Shutterstock.com; Cover, pp. 1, 3-80 STUDIO DREAM/Shutterstock.com; Cover, p. 1 HIGOOD/Shutterstock.com; p. 6 Johnstocker Production/Shutterstock.com; pp. 8, 40 Pressmaster/Shutterstock.com; pp. 10, 31 Rawpixel.com/Shutterstock.com; p. 12 New Africa/Shutterstock.com; p. 17 Alex Manders/Shutterstock.com; p. 18 https://commons.wikimedia.org/wiki/File:Sanfranciscoearthquake1906.jpg; p. 20 https://commons.wikimedia.org/wiki/File:Hooverville_on_the_Seattle_tideflats,_1933_(50495168952).jpg; p. 22 Steve Heap/Shutterstock.com; p. 25 Lightspring/Shutterstock.com; p. 28 Malivan_Iuliia/Shutterstock.com; p. 30 ChameleonsEye/Shutterstock.com; p. 33 SpeedKingz/Shutterstock.com; p. 35 Winthrop Brookhouse/Shutterstock.com; pp. 37, 47 Philip Pilosian/Shutterstock.com; p. 39 Ezume Images/Shutterstock.com; p. 43 Monkey Business Images/Shutterstock.com; p. 48 Dragana Gordic/Shutterstock.com; p. 50 Halfpoint/Shutterstock.com; p. 55 Wangkun Jia/Shutterstock.com; p. 57 Postmodern Studio/Shutterstock.com; p. 58 https://commons.wikimedia.org/wiki/File:Covenant_House_43_10_jeh.JPG; p. 60 SeventyFour/Shutterstock.com; p. 61 Darren Baker/Shutterstock.com; p 63 SewCream/Shutterstock.com; p. 65 Arthimedes/Shutterstock.com; p. 67 mangostock/Shutterstock.com.